Go Wild

BE AN ADVENTURER

Thanks to the creative team:
Senior Editor: Alice Peebles
Designer: Lauren Woods and collaborate agency

Original edition copyright 2015 by Hungry Tomato Ltd.

Copyright © 2016 by Lerner Publishing Group, Inc.

Hungry Tomato™ is a trademark of
Lerner Publishing Group, Inc.

Hungry Tomato™
A division of Lerner Publishing Group, Inc.
241 First Avenue North
Minneapolis, MN 55401 USA

For reading levels and more information, look up this title
at www.lernerbooks.com.

Main body text set in Zemke Hand ITC 14/1.7
Typeface provided by International Typeface Corporation

Library of Congress Cataloging-in-Publication Data

Oxlade, Chris.
    Be an adventurer / by Chris Oxlade ; illustrated by Eva Sassin.
      pages cm. — (Go wild)
    ISBN 978-1-4677-6357-8 (lb : alk. paper)
    ISBN 978-1-4677-7647-9 (pb : alk. paper)
    ISBN 978-1-4677-7222-8 (eb pdf)
    1. Adventure and adventurers—Juvenile literature. I. Sassin,
Eva, illustrator. II. Title.
    G525. 097 2016
    910.4—dc23   2015006262

Manufactured in the United States of America
1 – VP – 7/15/15

Go Wild

BE AN ADVENTURER

By Chris Oxlade
Illustrated by Eva Sassin

HUNGRY TOMATO™

Minneapolis

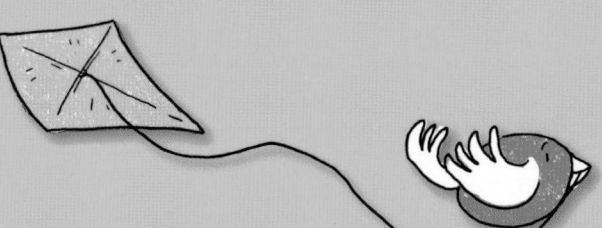

CONTENTS

TIME TO GO WILD

Where do you go to have adventures? Have you discovered the great outdoors? No? Then it's time to go wild! You can build a camp, make a raft, and have tons of fun. Even if you live in the middle of a city, you can have a wild time in your garden or your backyard, your local park, or another place where you have an adult's permission to explore.

Discover some of the skills you will need to have a great adventure in the wild: tying knots, building dams, sending messages, skimming stones, and even making a bow and arrow.

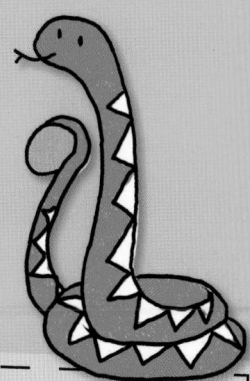

WILD SAFETY

- Never go exploring in the wild without an adult.
- Ask an adult before you do any of the projects in this book. In particular, ask before going near or in water, going to the coast, exploring in bad weather or in the dark, or using a GPS.

CARING FOR THE ENVIRONMENT

Always take care of the environment when you are in the wild. That means you:

- Never damage trees unless you are in a real emergency situation.
- Take special care to keep fires under control and make sure a fire is out before you leave it.

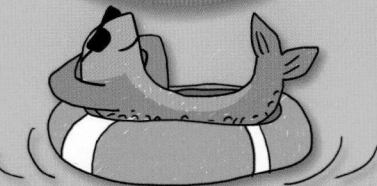

PACK YOUR GEAR

ADVENTURER'S EQUIPMENT

Every successful and exciting adventure starts with a little planning. That includes gathering all the adventure gear you might need. To start with, you'll need suitable clothing and ~~some~~ sturdy shoes or boots. The clothes you should take will depend on the weather. If it's roasting hot, you'll need cool clothes and a hat, and if it's raining or freezing cold, you'll need a waterproof, warm coat, a hat, and gloves.

An adventurer's pack

Here's a list of stuff to put in your backpack.

A pair of gloves

A hat

A waterproof jacket

A bivy bag (sleeping bag with covers)

A waterproof tarpaulin about 6 feet (2 m) square

Make sure you have a comfortable backpack with plenty of pockets.

KNIFE SAFETY

You'll need a knife to complete some of the projects in this book.

When using a knife, always:

- ask an adult first
- hold the knife firmly
- cut away from your body, arms, and legs, never towards them
- fold away or put away your knife whenever you are not using it
- ask an adult about the laws on owning and using a knife

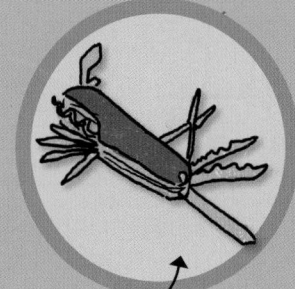

A multi-tool

High-energy emergency food, such as chocolate and nuts

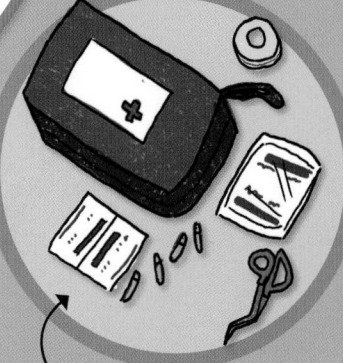

A small first-aid kit

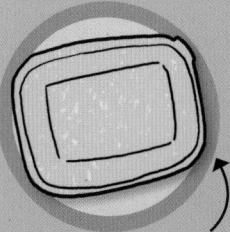

A survival kit (in a plastic container) with fire-lighting equipment, a needle and thread, a fishing line, a saw, and other useful items

Some paracord (strong multipurpose cord)

A mobile phone

A compass

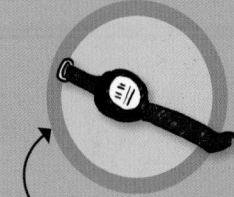

A watch

A map of where you are going

A small camera

Sunblock

A flashlight with spare batteries

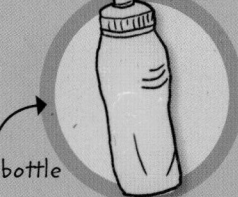

A water bottle

Insect repellent

Tent pegs

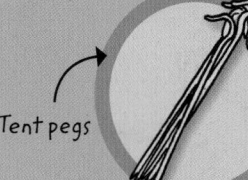

ROPE TRICKS

ADVENTURER'S KNOTS

It would be foolhardy to venture into the wild without knowing a few basic knots. Adventurers need knots for building shelters, making tools, and building rafts. So find a scrap of rope and start practicing.

A clove hitch

This is a knot for attaching a rope to a branch or pole. It is easy to undo. It's also handy when lashing branches together (see page 11). There are two ways to tie it.

Method 1: For a branch

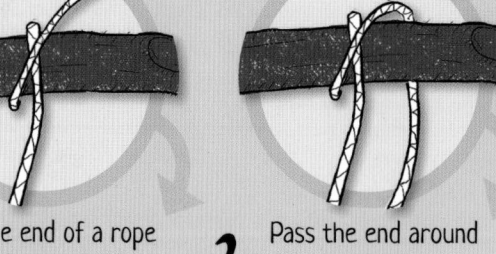

1. Pass the end of a rope over and around the branch, then over itself.

2. Pass the end around the branch again.

3. Thread the end under the second loop.

4. Pull tight.

Method 2: For a post

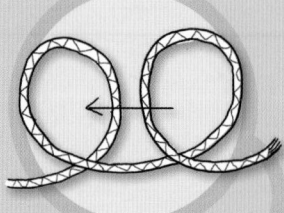

1. Form two loops near the end of the rope.

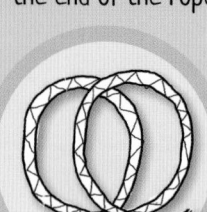

2. Place one loop over the other loop.

3. Drop the loops over a post and pull tight.

A bowline

Use this knot for attaching a rope to a thick tree or a fellow adventurer's waist.

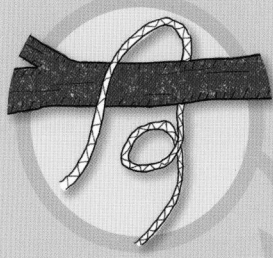

1. Pass the rope around the tree, then make a loop in the main rope.

2. Thread the end through the loop and around the main rope.

3. Thread the end back through the loop and pull tight.

A round turn and two half hitches

Use this strong knot for attaching a rope to a branch or post. It's also good for tying guy lines to trees or a boat to the shore.

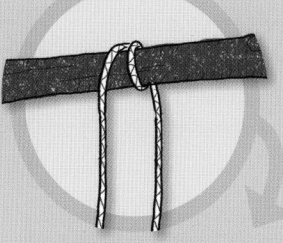

1. Wrap the end of the rope around the branch twice. (That's the "round turn.")

2. Pass the end under the main rope and back over itself.

3. Pull the rope tight. That's one "half hitch."

4. Repeat steps 2 and 3. That's two "half hitches."

These knots really work!

A figure-eight knot

This easy knot is useful for stopping a rope from sliding through a hole.

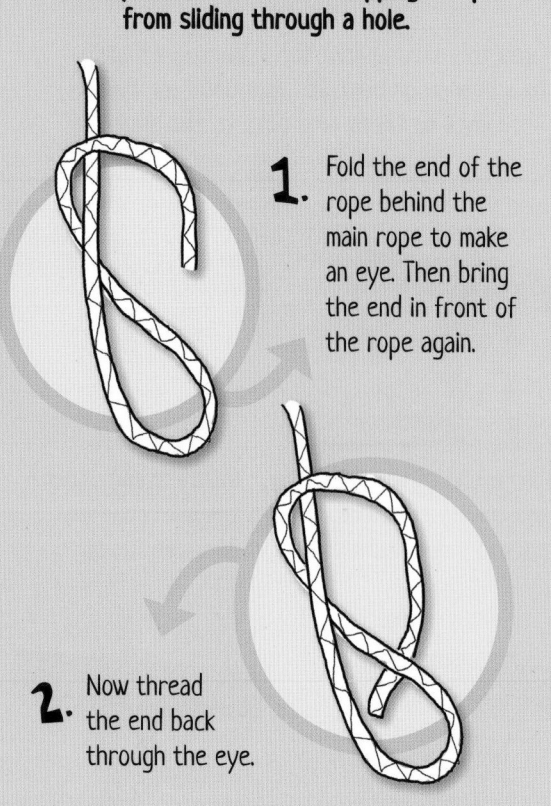

1. Fold the end of the rope behind the main rope to make an eye. Then bring the end in front of the rope again.

2. Now thread the end back through the eye.

3. Pull tight.

A reef knot

Use this knot to tie together two pieces of the same thickness of rope.

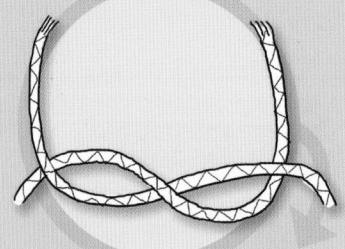

1. Pass the end of the right-hand rope over the left-hand rope, behind it, then over it again.

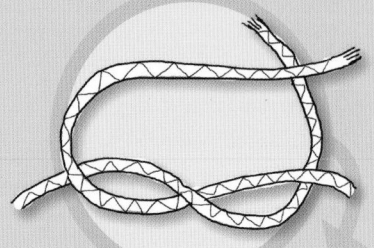

2. Pass the end of the right-hand rope over the end of the left-hand rope.

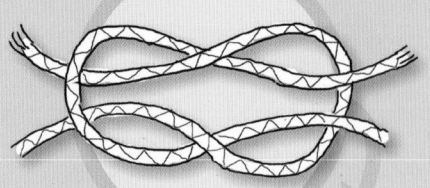

3. Thread the left-hand rope under the right-hand rope and pull tight.

Sigh!

10

A lashing

This knot is handy for tying two branches together at right angles to each other.

1. Place one branch over the other. Tie the end of the rope to the bottom branch with a clove hitch (see page 8).

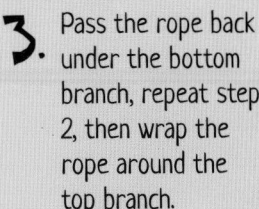

2. Pass the rope over the top branch, under the bottom branch, and back over the top branch.

3. Pass the rope back under the bottom branch, repeat step 2, then wrap the rope around the top branch.

4. Wind the rope twice around the ropes between the two branches.

5. Tie a clove hitch around the top branch to finish the knot.

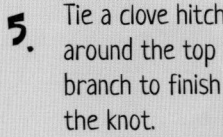

A sheet bend

Use this knot for tying a thick rope to a thin rope.

1. Bend over the end of the thick rope, then pass the thin rope through the bend.

2. Pass the thin rope around the back of the thick rope.

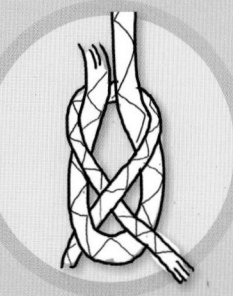

3. Thread the thin rope under itself and pull tight.

TAKE COVER!

MAKING A SHELTER

A tarp is a waterproof sheet. Tent groundsheets, plastic sheets, and builders' tarpaulins are all tarps. They are very versatile in the wild, especially for making shelters and rafts (see page 15).

A tarp tent

1. Make a frame by pushing two forked sticks, each about 3 feet (1 m) high, into the ground about 4.5 feet (2 m) apart. Find a stick long enough to rest in the forks.

2. You can also make a frame with two uprights and some paracord. Push two straight sticks, each about 3 feet (1 m) high, into the ground about 4.5 feet (2 m) apart. Push tent pegs or sticks into the ground in line with the uprights. Tie the paracord to the sticks with clove hitches (see page 8), then to the pegs.

4. Tie the pieces of paracord to tent pegs in the ground and tighten them.

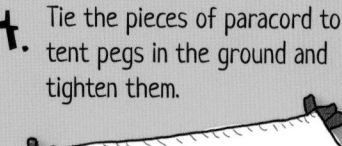

3. Put your tarp over the frame. If it has eyes in the corners, tie short pieces of paracord to them. If there are no eyes, fold a pebble into each corner of the tarp and hold it in place with a piece of paracord.

A tarp tunnel shelter

A tunnel shelter keeps out wind and rain better than a simple tarp shelter, but there's not as much space inside.

1. First make an A frame by lashing together two sticks about 3 ft (1 m) long (see page 10).

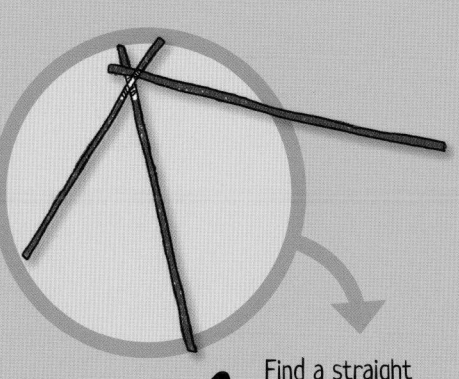

2. Find a straight branch about 6 feet (2 m) long and tie one end into the A frame with a lashing.

3. Put your tarp over the frame. Hold the edges down with rocks or logs.

Watch out for bears!

MORE SHELTER DESIGNS

Here are a couple more designs for tarp shelters. The first works with a small tarp, and the second gives you a dry place to lie down.

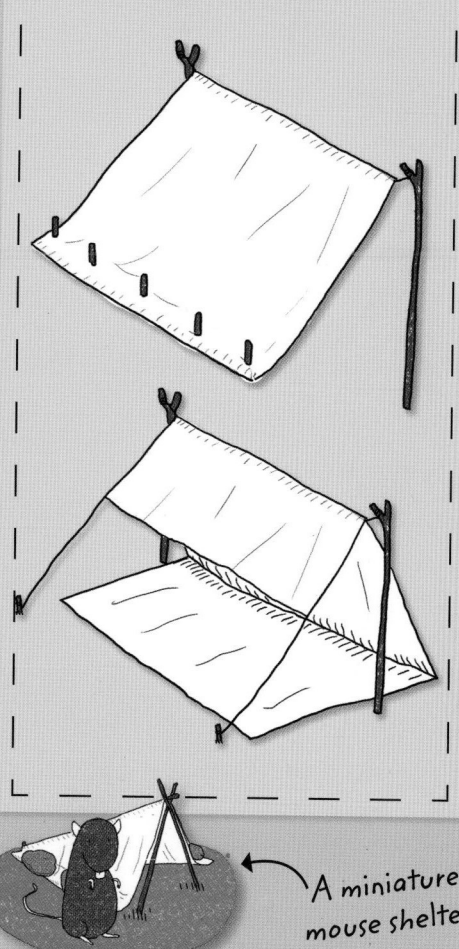

A miniature mouse shelter

FLOATING FUN

MAKING RAFTS

Imagine you are on an adventure and there's a deep river or a lake in your way. The only thing to do is to build yourself a raft. Try one of these simple designs:

Bottle raft

1. Collect lots of plastic bottles! You'll need about 30 2-liter bottles for this raft. Start arranging the bottles on a piece of thin board about 3 feet square (1 m).

2. Once the board is covered with bottles, attach the bottles to the board with strong tape, such as duct tape, or with cord. Secure the tape or cord right around the bottles and the board.

3. Grab a stick, sit on your raft, and paddle away!

RAFT SAFETY

Only use these rafts with adult supervision. Always wear a life jacket in water. Never go rafting on a fast-flowing river or in very cold water.

Watch out for piranha!

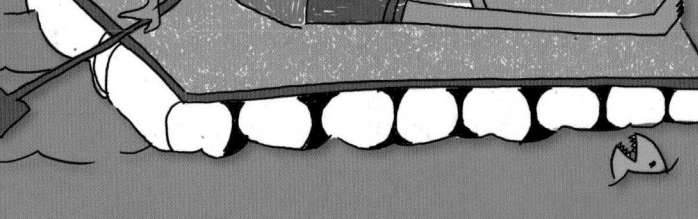

Doughnut Raft

1. Spread out a tarp that's about 6 feet square (2 sq. m)—one designed to make a shelter works well. Gather up bushy branches and arrange them into a doughnut shape on the tarp. Tie the branches together loosely with string or cord.

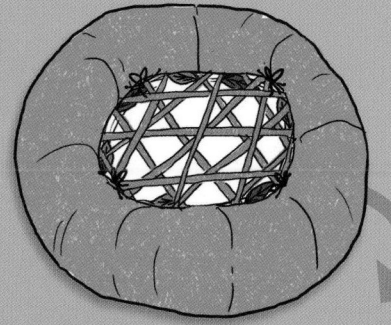

2. Fold the edges of the tarp into the center of the doughnut. Tuck the edges under the branches, or tie the edges together.

3. There should be a hole in the center for you to sit in, with your legs dangling over the side. Make sure you don't puncture the tarp! Paddle with a stick.

Log raft

!

1. Find six or more logs at least 4 inches (10 cm) across and at least 4 feet (1 m) long. **These will be heavy, so get an adult to help you collect them.**

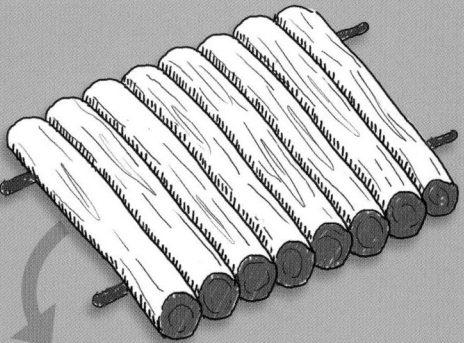

2. Place two strong sticks on the ground, about 6 feet (2 m) apart. Lay your logs side by side on top of the sticks. Now lay two more sticks on top of the logs above the first two sticks.

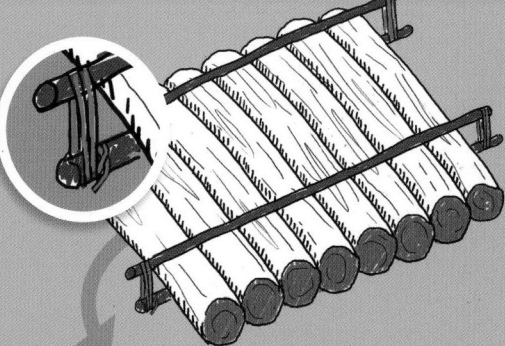

3. Tie the ends of the sticks together tightly with cord. Start with a clove hitch (see page 8) around one stick, then wind the cord around the sticks a few times and tie the loose end of the cord with another clove hitch.

SINK OR SWIM

WATERY HAZARDS

Out in the wild, there may not be a bridge for crossing a shallow stream or river, so you need the skills to get across safely. Be careful—it's not always easy to tell how deep the water is. If in doubt, don't cross.

RIVER SAFETY

Practice these skills crossing only small, shallow (that means ankle-deep) streams, and only under adult supervision. Never try to cross any stream or river that's more than knee-deep, or fast-flowing, or very wide. Flowing water is very powerful, and can easily sweep you off your feet.

Never cross a stream or a river where there are hazards such as rapids, waterfalls, or logjams, and avoid bends, where the water flows fast.

How to wade across a stream

1. If you have to cross a stream on your own, use a walking stick or pole to help you to balance. Face upstream and shuffle sideways. Move one foot at a time, making sure you get a good foothold.

2. This is one way to cross a stream in a group. Form a ring, so that two people can support you as you move your feet. Only one person moves at a time.

3. A group can also cross in a line, one behind the other, all facing upstream. The front person uses a stick for balance, and the others support him or her. Everybody moves slowly sideways, keeping in line.

Move this way

Water flow

How to escape from quicksand

If you are on a riverbank or a beach, you might blunder into quicksand. Follow these tips to escape. The same tricks work if you fall in a bog.

1. The first trick is to stay calm! Don't wriggle around! Keep still and you won't sink. Throw off your backpack to reduce your weight.

2. If you are only up to your knees, sit down. If you are in deeper, lean back, so that your weight is spread across the sand.

3. Now pull your legs out. Do this with very small movements, and very slowly! Then crawl to safety, keeping flat to spread out your weight.

WATER WALLS

BUILDING DAMS

You can build a dam across a stream to make a small pond, perhaps for cooling down with a swim or for catching fish. Make sure you're not breaking any laws or rules before you build a dam, and always dismantle your dam before you leave the area.

A stone dam

1. A stone dam needs to be wide at the base and narrow at the top, with sloping sides. Start by placing large rocks side by side, building a base 16–20 inches (40–50 cm) wide.

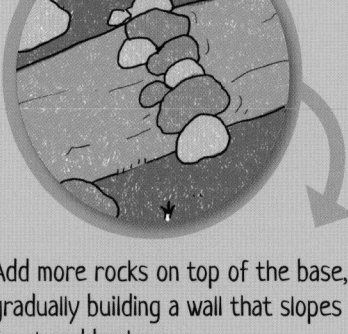

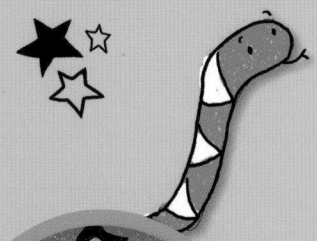

2. Add more rocks on top of the base, gradually building a wall that slopes front and back.

4. Push gravel or sand onto the back wall so that the water will wash it into the gaps. Wait for the water to build up behind your dam.

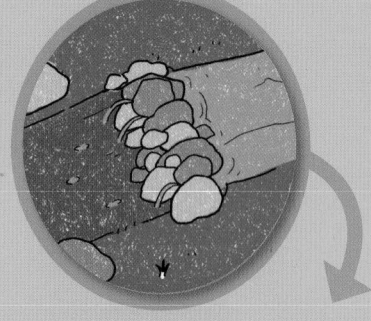

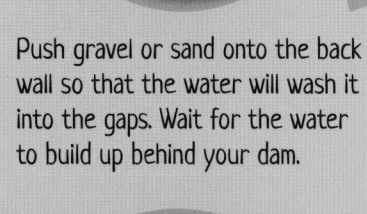

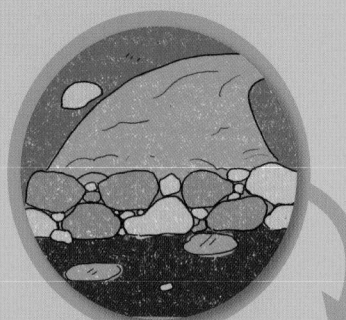

3. Water will leak through the gaps between the stones, so now find small stones to block the holes as well as you can. The water will help to push them into place.

5. Remember to knock down your dam before you go home.

A stick dam

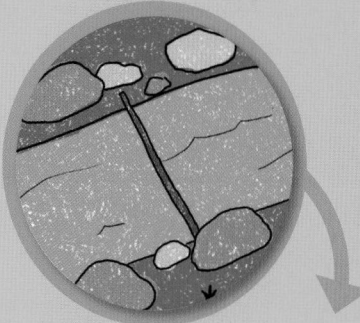

CHOOSING A DAM SITE
Only build a dam in a small, shallow stream — never in fast-flowing or deep water. A stream a few feet across, with a flat bed and high banks, is the easiest place to build a dam.

1. Find a branch long enough to stretch from one bank of the stream to the other. Stamp the ends down to help keep them in place.

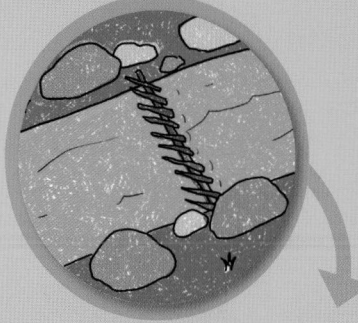

2. Find sticks to fit between the log and the stream bed. Angle them so their ends are further upstream then the log. Put the sticks as close together as you can.

Argh! Heavy!

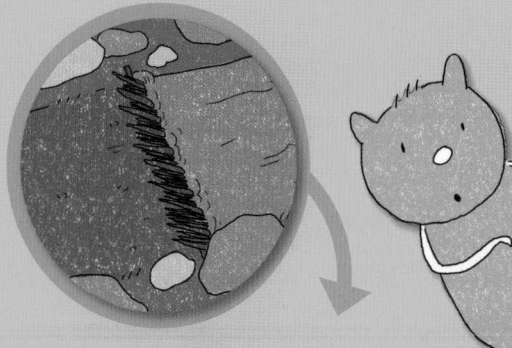

3. Add smaller sticks to fill the gaps between the larger sticks.

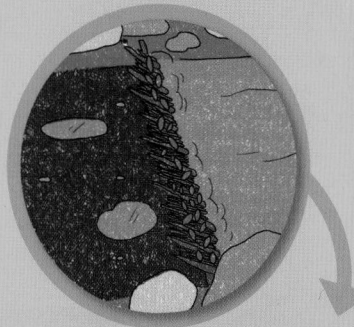

4. Finally, cover the sticks with leaves to block up any remaining gaps.

5. Wait for the water to build up behind your dam. Knock down your dam before you go home.

WILD SIGNS

SENDING MESSAGES

Out in the wild, your mobile phone probably won't get a signal, or its battery could go dead, or you could drop it in a river. No problem! There are other ways to send messages to your companions.

Signaling the way

You can leave signs on the ground to record your route or to show your companions the way you have gone.

Arrow made with rocks

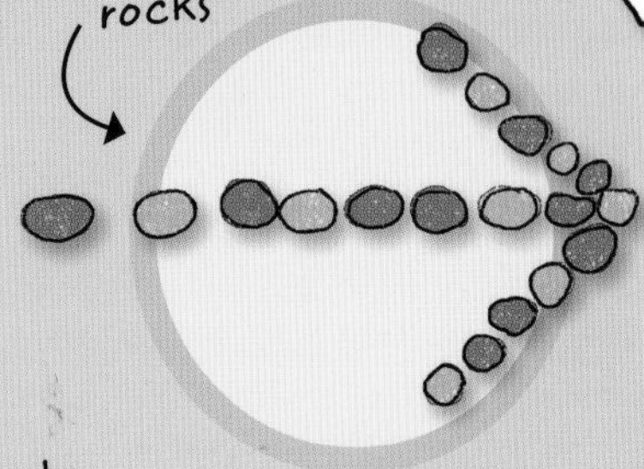

Pointing stick supported by forked stick

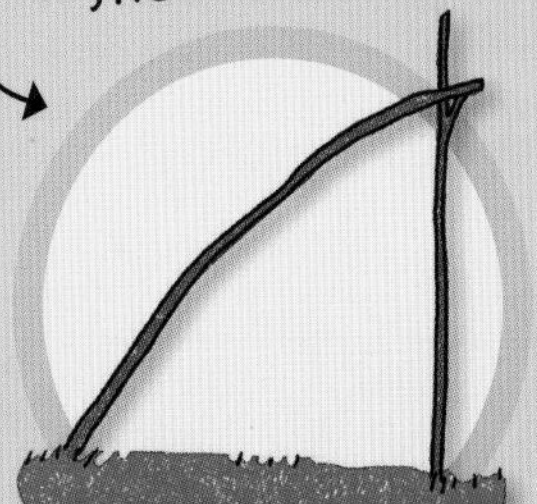

Arrow made with sticks

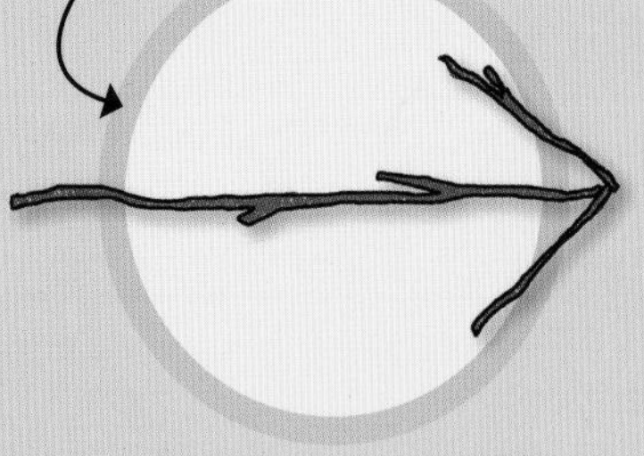

Arrow made with flour

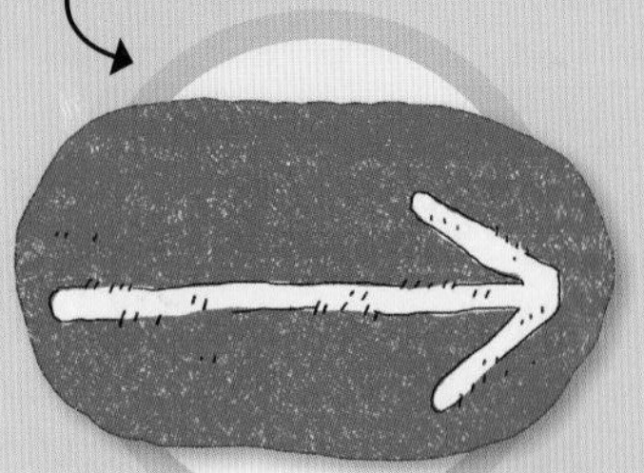

Hmmm, which way?

Spots of flour

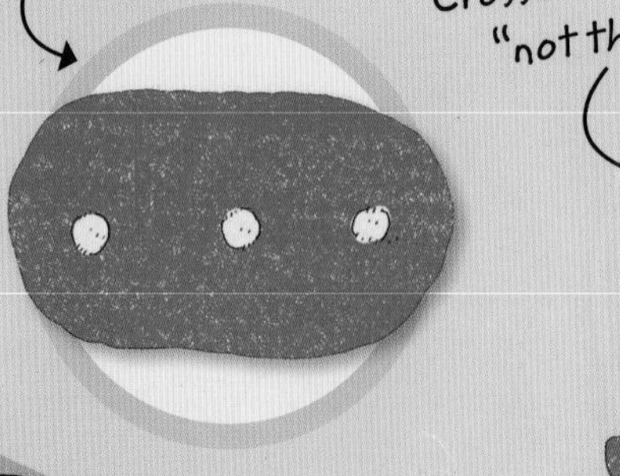

Crossed sticks mean "not this way"

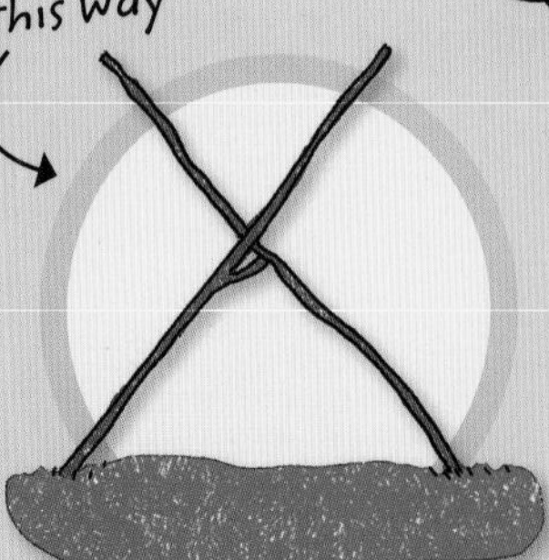

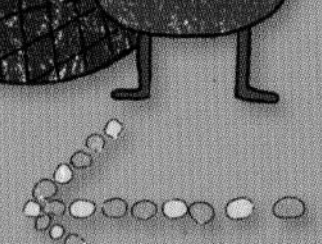

20

Morse code messages

Morse code is handy for sending messages to a companion who can't see you (so you use blasts of a whistle) or can't hear you (so you use flashes of a flashlight).

1. Look at the Morse code sheet (one of these could be a useful addition to your backpack). Try a simple emergency message. This is made up of the Morse code for the letters SOS: three short blasts or flashes, a small pause, then three long blasts or flashes, a small pause, and finally three more short blasts or flashes.

2. You can send any message you like using Morse code, as long as you and your companions know the code.

A ·—	J ·———	S ···
B —···	K —·—	T —
C —·—·	L ·—··	U ··—
D —··	M ——	V ···—
E ·	N —·	W ·——
F ··—·	O ———	X —··—
G ——·	P ·——·	Y —·——
H ····	Q ——·—	Z ——··
I ··	R ·—·	

0 —————	4 ····—	8 ———··
1 ·————	5 ·····	9 ————·
2 ··———	6 —····	
3 ···——	7 ——···	

Semaphore messages

Here's an alternative to Morse code if you lose your whistle and your flashlight!

1. You'll need two flags. You can make a flag by attaching a plastic bag to the end of a stick. Or use a leafy branch instead.

2. Study the semaphore code sheet here, then try sending some messages. Keep the messages short or your arms will soon get tired!

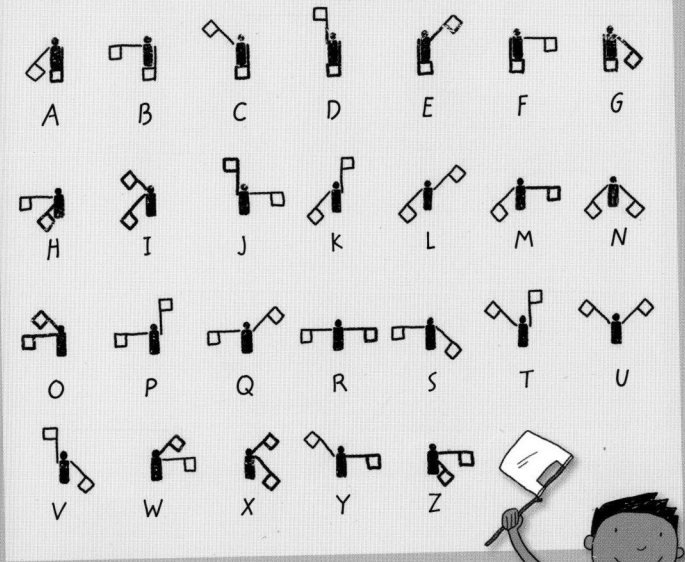

SLINGS AND SPLINTS

FIRST AID FOR ADVENTURERS

The occasional bump or scrape is part of being an adventurer. That's why you should always carry a first-aid kit. In an emergency, you might need to treat more serious injuries, such as broken bones or deep cuts. Here are some skills to practice on your uninjured friends.

FIRST-AID SAFETY

First aid is a great skill to have. It's best to learn from the experts by taking a certified first-aid course. If an accident does happen, get adult help as fast as you can. Never try out any first aid unless you know exactly what you are doing. You could make things worse.

Make a sling

A sling supports a broken arm or injured shoulder.

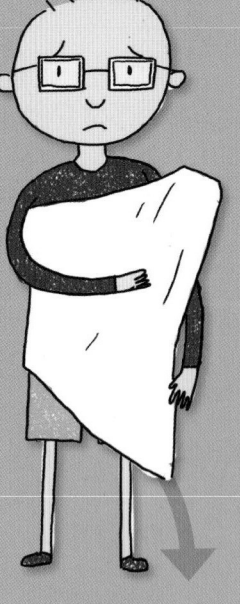
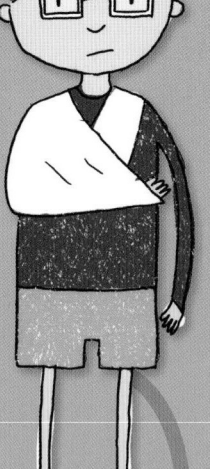

1. Open out a large triangular bandage and place it under the person's injured arm, with one end over the shoulder.

2. Lift the bottom corner up and over the shoulder and tie the ends together behind the neck.

3. Fold the edge around the elbow and fasten it with a safety pin.

Make a splint

Here's how to make an emergency splint for a broken leg.

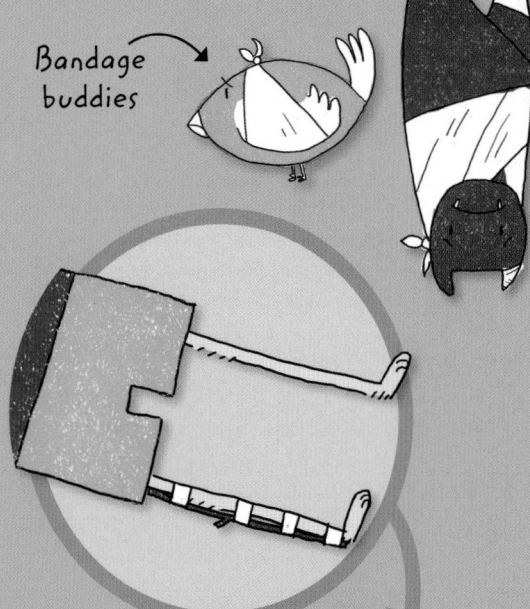

Bandage buddies

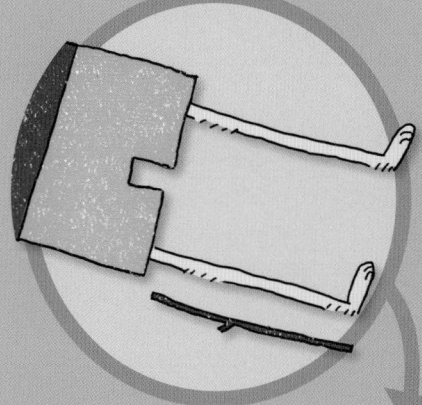

1. Ask the injured person to lie flat on the ground. Do not move the injured limb. Search for a strong stick about the same length as the person's leg. Place the stick alongside the injured leg.

2. Very gently and not too tightly, tie three or four bandages around the leg and the splint, above and below the injury. This will keep the leg still until help arrives.

Duct tape stitches

Wound with duct tape

All-purpose duct tape has many uses in the wild, including first aid. You can use it as an alternative to bandages for making slings and tying splints or use it to stitch a big cut.

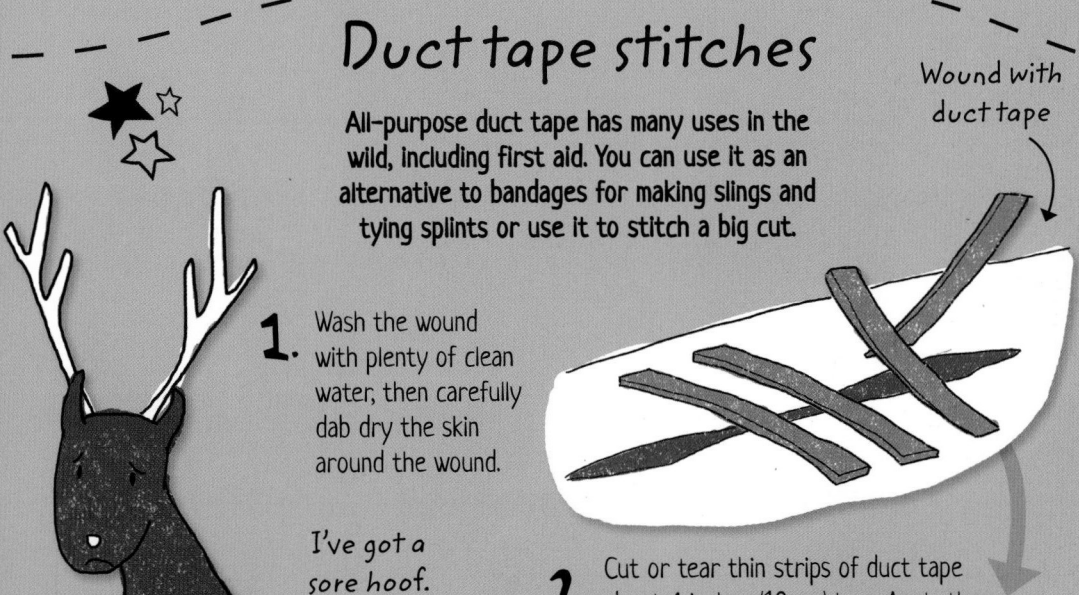

1. Wash the wound with plenty of clean water, then carefully dab dry the skin around the wound.

I've got a sore hoof.

2. Cut or tear thin strips of duct tape about 4 inches (10 cm) long. Apply them across the wound, pressing the wound gently together as you do.

Charcoal medicine

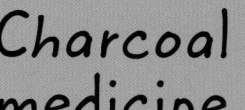

In an emergency, charcoal (not ashes) from the burned sticks in a cold campfire can help to settle an upset stomach and can also help to counteract poison.

1. Make sure the fire is cold. Take a burned stick and use another stick to scrape off the black charcoal into a container or onto a piece of bark.

2. Eat the charcoal with plenty of water, but don't eat too much. A spoonful is enough. Did you know that charcoal can also be used to filter water to make it clean?

Muddy sunblock

You should always carry some sunblock in your backpack to prevent painful sunburn. If you run out, there is an alternative: mud! It's a trick that some animals use.

Find a source of good, thick mud. Clay is best, and you can add water if you need to. Muddy soil doesn't work so well.

Maggot therapy

We know it sounds disgusting. But in the wild, maggots will clean an infected wound by eating away damaged flesh. Obviously, we're not suggesting you try this on a grazed knee. You'd only need it for a deep and dirty wound in a real emergency, when no other first aid is available and when you have adult supervision.

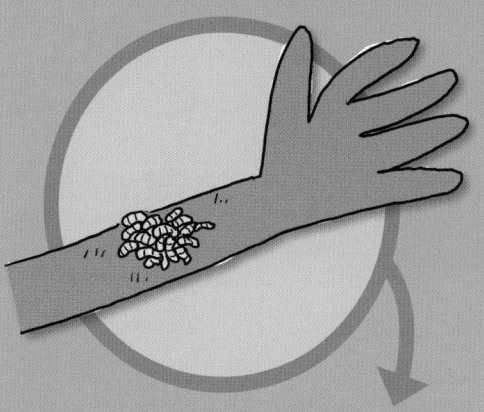

1. Leave the wound open to the air for a day, so that flies can lay eggs in it. Ugh!

2. Cover the wound. Check it each day, and you should find maggots. Even more ugh!

3. When the wound looks clean (without any pus or dirt), wash away the maggots with fresh water and bandage it up with a clean dressing.

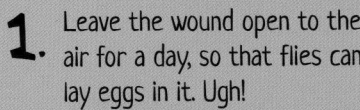

Make an emergency stretcher

Here's how to make a stretcher to carry an injured companion to safety.

1. Find two strong branches, each about 6 feet (2 m) long. These should be stiff but not too heavy.

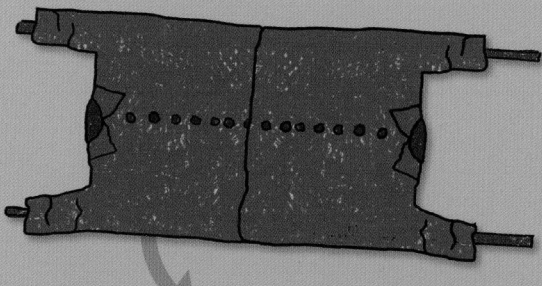

2. Turn the sleeves of two coats inside out and push the logs through them.

Don't always trust bears to carry your stretcher.

I'll lead the way!

ADVENTURE FUN AND GAMES

Going on an adventure is not all about racing around in the woods, crossing streams, and building shelters, rafts, and dams. Sometimes you have to stop for a rest. Then you can play a few games and have some fun.

Skimming a stone

Impress your friends by being a champion stone skimmer.

1. The best stones for skimming are flat, about 4 inches (10 cm) across and about 0.5 inches (1 cm) thick.

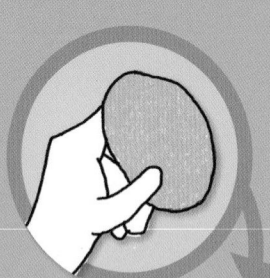

2. You need to grip the stone correctly for a good skim. Place your index finger behind the stone, your thumb on top, and the other fingers underneath.

3. Stand sideways to the water and bend your knees to get low to the water. Pull your arm back, keeping the stone horizontal. Now throw the stone forwards, releasing it so that your index finger makes it spin.

4. Your stone should fly low across the water, land a few yards from you, and skim along.

Skimming snake

Make a kite

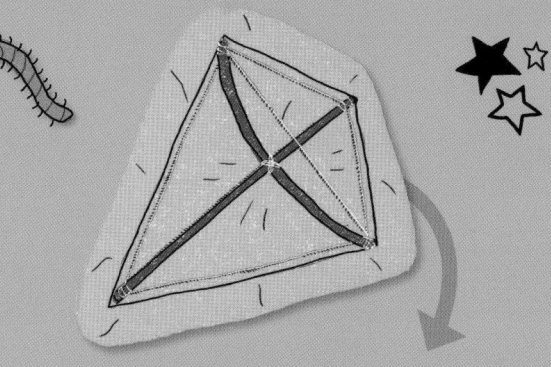

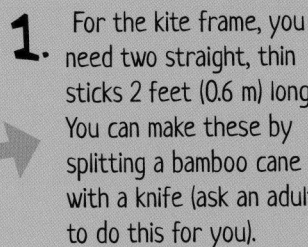

1. For the kite frame, you need two straight, thin sticks 2 feet (0.6 m) long. You can make these by splitting a bamboo cane with a knife (ask an adult to do this for you).

2. Carefully cut a notch 0.5 inches (1 cm) from each end of both sticks.

3. Tie the sticks together, with the center of one stick 4 inches (10 cm) along the other stick, to make a cross.

4. Tie string tightly from one end of the crossbar to the other, using the notches, to make it slightly bowed.

5. Tie string around the outside of the frame, using the notches to keep it in place. Try to keep each part of the string taut. Now place the frame on a piece of plastic from a plastic bag.

6. Cut out the plastic, leaving about 1 inch (3 cm) outside the frame. Then fold the edges of the plastic over and tape them down.

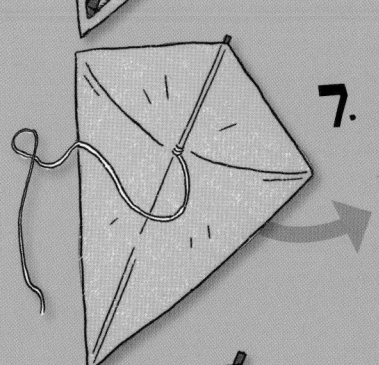

7. Tie a string between the cross and the base to act as a tether.

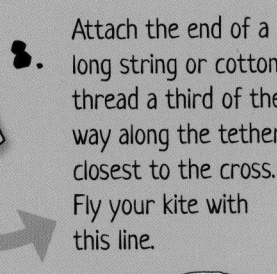

8. Attach the end of a long string or cotton thread a third of the way along the tether, closest to the cross. Fly your kite with this line.

Make a bow and arrow

Create a bow and arrows from the sticks you find in the wild. Ask an adult to help you make the bow and to supervise when you are firing arrows. Never fire at a person or an animal.

1. Find a bendy stick about 6 feet (2 m) long for your bow (not a dead stick, which could break). Cut off any side branches and smooth the stick with a knife.

2. Carefully cut a V-shaped notch at each end of the bow. These should point towards the center.

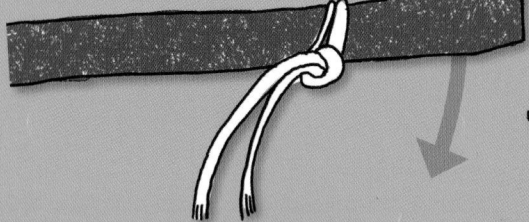

3. Cut a length of string about 3 feet (1 m) longer than the bow. Tie one end of the string to one end of the bow, using a round turn and two half hitches (see page 9).

4. Stretch the string to the other end of the bow, using your weight to keep it slightly bent. Ask an adult to help you with this step. Tie the string to the end of the bow with a round turn and two half hitches.

5. Now make an arrow. Find a thin stick about 2 feet (0.6 m) long. Carve one end to make it pointed, but not sharp. Carve the other end to make it flat. Cut a notch in this end.

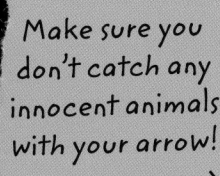

Make sure you don't catch any innocent animals with your arrow!

6. Stick three pieces of duct tape together close to the blunt end to make feathers. Trim the feathers to make them narrow.

8. Hold the bow upright and pull back on the string until the point of the arrow is close to the bow. Make sure all humans and animals are out of the way before you fire.

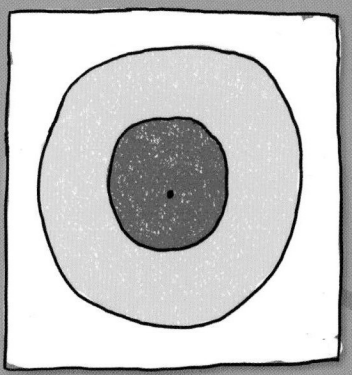

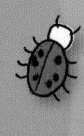

7. It's time to fire an arrow. Hold the bow with your left hand. Put the notch in the arrow over the string and let the arrow rest on the thumb of your left hand. Hold the string with two fingers.

9. Aim your arrow at something—such as a paper target pinned to a tree—and release!

DID YOU KNOW?

O Knots are often named after the job they used to do. The bowline was used to tie the corner of a sail to the bow of a ship, and a reef knot was used to reef a sail (reduce its area).

O In 1947 Norwegian adventurer Thor Heyerdahl and his crew sailed 4,300 miles (6,900 kilometers) across the Pacific Ocean in 101 days, on a raft made from balsa wood tree trunks. The raft was called *Kon-Tiki.*

O In 2008 two sailors traveled from California to Hawaii on a raft called *JUNK,* made from plastic pop bottles. The sailors wanted to highlight the problem of the millions of plastic bottles floating in the world's oceans.

Excuse me, but do you know you are on the sand?

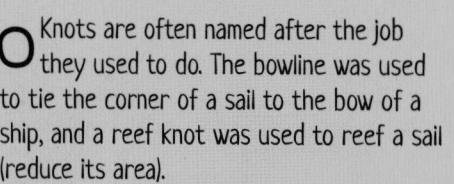

You really should be wearing a life jacket like me!

O If there's no bridge to cross a river, and you don't want to wade across, how about walking a tightrope? Jay Cochrane walked 2,098 feet (639 meters) on a tightrope 1,340 feet (408 meters) above the Yangtze River in China.

O Despite what you might think, you can't sink completely in quicksand, because your body would float. But you can get trapped in quicksand, so it's dangerous, especially if you are caught on a beach when the tide is rising.

O Beavers are amazing natural dam builders. They construct dams from logs and branches to create deep pools in rivers. The biggest beaver dam ever found was 930 yards (850 meters) long. It was spotted in Canada on satellite photographs.

American inventor Samual Morse created Morse code in 1884 to send messages along a telegraph wire. The code uses a combination of long and short pulses of electricity (or light or sound) to represent letters. The first message ever sent by Morse code was, "What hath God wrought?"

One of the earliest distress messages sent by Morse code was from the RMS *Titanic* as it sank.

Semaphore was designed by the French Chappe brothers in the late eighteenth century, to send messages between French army units. Their system used huge mechanical arms on hilltop towers to relay messages across France.

The World Stone Skimming Championships are held every year in Scotland. The world record skim is 51 skips, covering 250 feet (76 meters), achieved by American Russell Byars in 2007.

The best wood for making bows comes from yew trees, so if you can find some yew wood, use it for a bow!

Modern bows are composite, which means they are made from different materials combined in layers, such as wood and carbon fiber.

The farthest an arrow has ever been fired from a bow is 1,336 yards (1,222 meters). The arrow was shot by an American named Don Brown in 1987.

I think my stone is a bit too big.

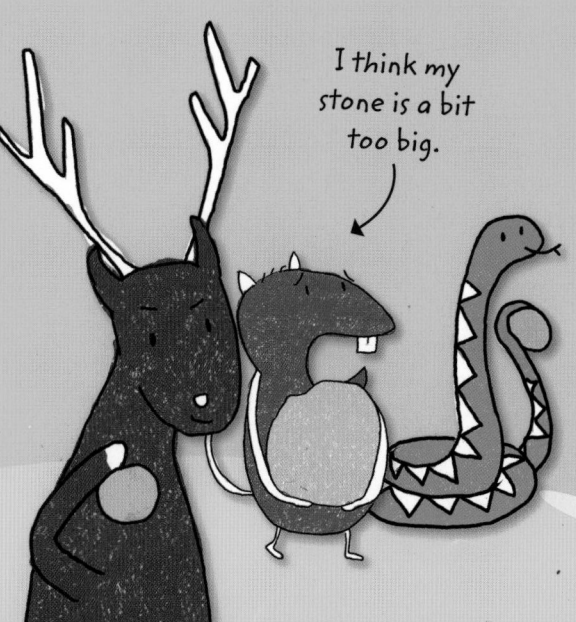

The first annual ANIMAL world stone skimming championships.

INDEX

THE AUTHOR

Chris Oxlade is an experienced author of educational books for children. He has written more than two hundred books on science, technology, sports, and hobbies, including many activity and project books. He enjoys camping and adventurous outdoor sports including rock climbing, hill running, kayaking, and sailing. He lives in England with his wife, children, and dogs.

THE ARTIST

Eva Sassin is a freelance illustrator born and bred in London, England. She has loved illustrating ever since she can remember, and she loves combining characters with unusual textures to give them more depth and keep them interesting.